Zachary Taylor

Zachary Taylor

Deborah Kops

AMERICA'S
12TH
PRESIDENT

Children's Press®
A Division of Scholastic Inc.
New York / Toronto / London / Auckland / Sydney
Mexico City / New Delhi / Hong Kong
Danbury, Connecticut

Library of Congress Cataloging-in-Publication Data

Kops, Deborah.
  Zachary Taylor / by Deborah Kops.
   p. cm. — (Encyclopedia of presidents. Second series)
  Summary: A biography of the twelfth president of the United States, with
information on his childhood, family, political career, presidency, and legacy.
Includes bibliographical references and index.
  ISBN 0-516-23442-0
  1. Taylor, Zachary, 1784–1850—Juvenile literature. 2. Presidents—United
States—Biography—Juvenile literature. [1. Taylor, Zachary, 1784–1850. 2.
Presidents.] I. Title. II. Series.

E422.K66 2003
973.6'3'092—dc22   2003015962

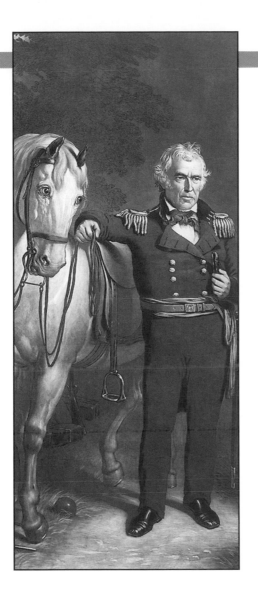

Contents

One   7
The Frontier Boy Becomes a Soldier

Two   19
Fighting on the Home Front

Three   37
The Hero of Buena Vista

Four   53
The People's Candidate for President

Five   65
Taylor's Presidency

Six   89
Taylor's Legacy

Presidential Fast Facts   96
First Lady Fast Facts   97
Timeline   98
Glossary   100
Further Reading   101
Places to Visit   102
Online Sites of Interest   103
Table of Presidents   104
Index   108

Chapter 1

The Frontier Boy Becomes a Soldier

Old Rough-and-Ready

On February 23, 1847, General Zachary Taylor was nearly surrounded. Commanding a force of 5,000 U.S. troops, he was defending a rugged mountain pass in northern Mexico against a Mexican army of nearly 20,000. In the past year, he had become a hero in the United States. He had driven Mexican forces out of disputed territory in Texas and had captured the important Mexican town of Monterrey. Now it seemed that all those victories would be for nothing.

When Taylor learned that the huge Mexican force was approaching, he had chosen this strong defensive position at a hacienda (a ranch or estate) called Buena Vista, near Monterrey. For two days, Santa Anna, the Mexican commander, had made one attack after another, hoping to destroy Taylor's force. As usual, Taylor was cool under fire, moving from one position to another and encouraging his men with little concern for his own safety. They sometimes referred to the heavyset, plain-looking general by his nickname, "Old Rough-and-Ready."

Taylor's men fought brilliantly that day, holding off each attack, but they were exhausted as they bedded down for the night. Tired as they were, few of them could sleep. The mountain air was cold, and there were no blankets or fires to warm them. All around them, wolves were howling. When dawn finally came, the Americans expected another day of bitter fighting. They were amazed to discover that the Mexican army had fled, leaving Buena Vista and all of northern Mexico under U.S. control. Taylor hugged one of his commanders with relief.

When word of Taylor's victory at Buena Vista reached the city of New Orleans, two fast horses rushed the news across the country to Washington and other major cities. With the help of the recently invented telegraph, every town and village in the United States soon heard the glad tidings. Now Taylor was a true national hero. Many people wanted to express their gratitude by electing him president. A few months later, a New Yorker wrote, "I have seen on the ice carts, and other vehicles drawn about the city the portrait of General Taylor well painted on the tailboard. . . . It is on the butcher's stall, it is on the market places."

Sam Chamberlain, who fought at Buena Vista, later painted this watercolor showing the eerie, cold battlefield at night.

Could "Old Rough-and-Ready" get elected? If he became president, would he be as effective in the White House as he was on the battlefield? Only time would tell.

Child of the Frontier ———————————

Zachary Taylor was born in Virginia on November 24, 1784. The Taylors were a distinguished family with large estates and a long history of public service. When Zachary was only eight months old, however, his parents and two older brothers left their comfortable way of life and traveled across the Appalachian Mountains to present-day Kentucky (which was then a far western possession of Virginia).

Two things encouraged Zachary's father, Richard, to move west to the frontier. First, he was a younger son. According to Virginia's laws of inheritance, most of the Taylors' plantations and thousands of acres of land would pass to the oldest son, leaving only a small parcel for Richard. Second, Richard had fought for the American colonies during the American Revolution. As pay for his services as a soldier, he had received 8,000 acres (3,200 hectares) of land in the unsettled territory across the mountains. That land would give him a good start.

The family probably crossed the mountains at the Cumberland Gap. On the western side, they would reach the Monongahela River, and travel downstream by flatboat to the Ohio River in Pennsylvania. From there, the Ohio travels south and west. The Taylors stopped at the lovely rapids called the Falls of the Ohio, in the small settlement of Louisville. Their home, which they called Springfield, was a large, rolling tract of wilderness east of town on the Beargrass Creek.

For the next eight years, Zachary lived in a small log cabin with his parents and two older brothers, Hancock and William. When he was six, his brother George was born, and two years later, his sister Elizabeth arrived. Although there were probably no other houses in sight, Zachary's childhood wasn't lonely. His friend George Croghan lived on the farm next to Springfield. About 80 miles (130 kilometers) away, in the town of Lexington, lived his cousins and his uncle, Captain Zachary Taylor Jr., who had fought with George Washington during the American Revolution. In 1792, before Zachary turned eight, Kentucky separated from Virginia and was admitted as the 15th state in the United States.

Zachary did not have much formal education. He and his friend George studied with two teachers. The first was a traveling schoolteacher from Connecticut who rode between New England and the frontier on his mule, setting up school wherever he happened to be. The second was a more accomplished scholar from Ireland. Despite his meager education, Zachary learned to write reasonably well, though he had a little trouble with spelling.

Like other children on the frontier, Zachary spent much of his time learning practical things by helping to clear and farm the land and manage a quickly growing plantation. He also learned to face danger. Wolves and wildcats roamed

The old Taylor homestead near Beargrass Creek in Louisville. This photograph was taken in the 1920s.

the forests. More threatening were Native Americans, who still hunted in the forests. From their point of view, the settlers were stealing valuable hunting territory, and they sometimes attacked an isolated farm or settlement. A neighbor, Mrs. Chenoweth, liked to tease Zachary and his playmates by showing them her bald head, which had been scalped by the Indians. Life on the frontier tended to make settlers tough. It was a good training ground for the future hero of Buena Vista.

Lieutenant Taylor

By the time Zachary was 20, in 1804, he and his family were living in a comfortable brick house large enough for his parents and their eight children. Native Americans no longer raided the settlements around Louisville, and this meant that Richard Taylor could spend more time managing his growing estate. As he brought more land under cultivation, Springfield, the Taylors' farm, became more like the plantations in Virginia. By 1804, Richard Taylor had about 30 slaves, making him one of the largest slave owners in the region. He was also buying land in other parts of the state. In addition to Springfield, he owned more than 10,000 acres (4,000 ha) of land in seven counties. Richard Taylor was also a leader in the community. He served at various times as justice of the peace, county magistrate (judge), and tax collector. Zachary learned the value of public service early in his life.

Slavery in the United States in the Early 1800s

When Zachary Taylor was a young man, slavery was already becoming an issue that divided the United States. Many thoughtful people saw a contradiction between the American ideal that "all men are created equal" and the enslavement of African Americans. By 1800 slavery had been outlawed in the northern states of Vermont, Massachusetts, and New Hampshire. In Pennsylvania, Connecticut, and Rhode Island, children born to slaves were freed at birth.

Some slave owners in Maryland, Virginia, and North Carolina freed children born to slaves or left wills freeing their slaves. President George Washington arranged for hundreds of slaves on his Virginia plantation to be freed after he and his wife had died. Like others in his region, Washington was growing less tobacco, a crop that required lots of attention and hard work that only slaves were available to do. Instead, he was growing cereal grains such as wheat and corn, which required less labor. If these trends had continued, slavery might have died out gradually.

The continuing need for slaves was tied to raising cotton. Planters in the states of the Deep South found that there was a strong market for the fiber, which made sturdy and durable cloth. Then in 1793, Eli Whitney invented the cotton gin ("gin" is short for "engine"). This simple machine, operated by a crank, made it easy to remove seeds from a cotton boll, allowing one worker to process more cotton in a day than a dozen workers could process by hand. This made it possible to process huge crops of short-fiber cotton for sale to cloth-makers in Great Britain and around the world. The problem was that growing cotton required as much attention and hard work as growing tobacco. As plantation owners grew more cotton, they needed more and more slaves to plant it, cultivate it, and harvest it.

Thanks to the enormous demand in Britain for southern cotton, the economy of the Deep South was booming. Zachary Taylor wanted to participate in the prosperity, and he eventually bought cotton plantations in Louisiana. By the time he ran for president, he had 145 slaves.

Picking cotton was a backbreaking job that required bending and stooping and carrying baskets long distances.

Louisville offered pleasant distractions for a young man living on the frontier. Thanks to its location on the banks of the Ohio River, it had grown into a busy river town of about 700 residents, including lawyers, doctors, and prosperous merchants. For the young in years or in spirit, private parties and balls offered festive entertainment. Taylor "cut" pigeonwings and "trotted" jigs, as the dances of the day were called, with the best of them.

Taylor knew, however, that soon he would have to find a way to earn a living. As a younger son like his father, he would not inherit most of Richard Taylor's plantations or land. An opportunity arrived in the spring of 1808. As a result of tensions between the United States and both England and France, Congress greatly increased the size of the army. Taylor applied for a commission as an officer in the U.S. Army. With the help of his father and other influential relatives, the 23-year-old Kentuckian was appointed first lieutenant of the 7th Infantry Regiment.

The army was a logical career choice for Taylor. Like many incoming officers, he was from a prosperous family and would not have to rely completely on the small salary the army paid. The position required practical talents and leadership, but not much formal education.

Taylor's first assignment was to set up an army recruiting station in Maysville, Kentucky, northeast of Louisville on the Ohio River. It was a good

Margaret Mackall Smith Taylor.

place to find new settlers, strong men who might be interested in joining the army, but he missed the active social life of Louisville. As Taylor wrote to his father, "I am rather badly off here on the score of society."

In the fall of 1809, during a visit to Louisville, Taylor met a slender young woman named Margaret Mackall Smith, who was visiting her sister at the time. "Peggy," the daughter of a prominent Maryland plantation owner, welcomed the attentions of the lieutenant. The Taylors were a respected family, and Peggy may have liked Zachary's striking army uniform, with its gold-trimmed cuffs and collar. Modest and very competent, she would learn to manage a family on her own when Zachary was away on military duty. The two were married on June 21, 1810, in a log cabin near Taylor's father's estate. Taylor was 25 and Peggy was about four years younger. For a wedding gift, Taylor's father gave the couple 324 acres (130 ha) of farmland on Beargrass Creek.

Chapter 2

The War of 1812 —————————

In April 1812, the United States seemed very close to a war with Great Britain. Taylor, who had been promoted to captain, received new orders. The British and their Native American allies were threatening forts and settlements along the frontier in the Indiana Territory. Taylor was ordered to form a company of men and travel to Fort Harrison. Because the government didn't have adequate transportation or supplies on the frontier, he spent $59 of his own money to supply and transport 50 men to the fort. It was a hefty sum. The Kentucky captain received only $40 a month, and he had a growing family to support. The Taylors' first child, Ann Mackall, was almost a year old.

Not long after Taylor and his men arrived at Fort Harrison, on the Wabash River, the United States declared war on Great Britain. Almost immediately, several military posts on the northwestern frontier fell to the British. The British were not the only threat to Fort

Fast Facts

THE WAR OF 1812

Who: The United States and Great Britain

When: The U.S. declared war in June 1812. The Treaty of Ghent ended the war in December 1814, but fighting continued into January 1815.

Why: Britain interfered with U.S. traders. It stopped U.S. ships, took cargo, and impressed American seamen—forced them to serve in the British navy. The British also kept forts in the Old Northwest and supported Native American attacks on U.S. settlements.

Where: The United States and Canada, and on the Atlantic Ocean. U.S. invasions of British Canada failed. In 1813 the U.S. navy defeated a British fleet on Lake Erie, leading to land victories at Detroit and the Thames River in Canada. In 1814 the British captured Washington, D.C., and burned public buildings, but were defeated soon afterward at Baltimore. After the treaty was signed, a British force was defeated at New Orleans by a U.S. force led by Andrew Jackson in January 1815.

Outcome: The Treaty of Ghent left boundaries as they were before the war. Britain made concessions on impressment of U.S. seamen and gave up forts south of the Great Lakes, opening western lands to the Mississippi River to U.S. settlement.

Harrison, however. Tecumseh, a leader of the Shawnee people, was organizing raids on U.S. forts in the Northwest. He had been encouraging American Indians in the region to resist white settlement of their lands. Now, supported by the British, he could attack the army's frontier defenses.

On September 4, 1812, two guards at Fort Harrison heard some Indians exchanging turkey-call signals in the woods nearby. Since more than half of the soldiers were sick, two civilians offered to go investigate. They never returned. That night a few Indians sneaked into the fort and started a fire. As the fire spread to the barracks, the Shawnee attacked.

Zachary Taylor, who was sick himself, was shocked at the cowardly behavior of his recruits. "Most of the men immediately gave

Fort Harrison in 1812, on a hill overlooking the Wabash River. The site is near present-day Terre Haute, Indiana.

themselves up for lost," Taylor reported later, "and I had the greatest difficulty in getting my orders executed." Taylor managed to organize his men so that most could hold off the Indians shooting at the fort, while a few, ducking musket balls, put out the fire. By early morning, the attack was over. For his bravery and leadership, Taylor received a brevet, or temporary promotion, to major.

The war continued for two more years, but Taylor saw only limited action. The conflict was ended by the Treaty of Ghent, signed on December 24, 1814. Before word of the treaty reached the United States, a British force marched on New Orleans, near the mouth of the Mississippi River. General Andrew Jackson assembled a smaller force of regulars and volunteers. On January 8, 1815, Jackson's troops inflicted heavy casualties on the British and forced them to retreat. For his victory at New Orleans, Jackson became a national hero and was later elected president. Taylor, a junior officer stationed along the western frontier in present-day Indiana and Illinois, had few chances to show his military skills.

A Home Base in Baton Rouge

Soon after the war ended, Congress voted to reduce the size of the U.S. army. Many officers were discharged from the service. Taylor learned that he could remain in the army, but only at the rank of captain. Discouraged by being demoted and by the reduction in pay, Taylor resigned. Respect from colleagues and superiors was very important to the proud officer from Kentucky. He decided to try his hand at farming his property on Beargrass Creek.

He soon learned that farming gave him little satisfaction. "It affords nothing sufficiently interesting to trouble my friends by communicating with them on the subject," he grumbled to a cousin. By that time, his daughter, Ann, had a new sister, Sarah Knox. Another daughter, Octavia, was born in 1816. A fourth daughter, Margaret, was born in 1819.

In 1816 Taylor got a chance to return to the army. He was offered a commission as a major in the 3rd Infantry and gladly accepted. He was stationed first in the Michigan Territory and later in Louisiana. There Zachary and Peggy Taylor experienced a family tragedy. In the fall of 1820, Peggy and the four Taylor daughters went to stay with Peggy's sister in Bayou Sara, Louisiana, while Taylor was away supervising a road construction project. The family came down with a disease then called "bilious fever." Octavia, not quite four years old, died. Taylor rushed to Bayou Sara to comfort his family.

Taylor returned to his post, but learned soon after that his wife Peggy was very sick. Deeply upset by the news, he wrote a military friend, "This information has nearly unmanned me, for my loss will be an irreparable one." Peggy recovered, but Margaret, the baby of the family, died. It was a second hard blow to the family.

The Pentagon Barracks in Baton Rouge were being built to house troops when Zachary Taylor was stationed there. Today they are part of the Louisiana State Capitol grounds and are used as offices and apartments.

In November 1822, Taylor, now a lieutenant colonel, was assigned to the 1st Infantry's main base in Baton Rouge, Louisiana. Peggy joined Taylor on this stretch of high ground above the Mississippi River surrounded by plantations. Taylor liked it so well that he bought a 380-acre (150-ha) cotton plantation nearby for $6,000 and moved 22 slaves from his land in Kentucky to cultivate his crops. For the rest of his life, Zachary Taylor considered Baton Rouge his home. Two more children were born to the Taylors in the 1820s. Mary Elizabeth, known as Betty, came along in 1824. Two years later, a long-awaited son, Richard, was born.

Back to the Northwest ——————————

The life of a career army officer brought frequent moves. In 1828 Taylor was assigned to the upper Mississippi region, where he and his family would live for nearly ten years. His first assignment was the command of Fort Snelling, on a steep bank of the Mississippi River between the present-day cities of Minneapolis and Saint Paul, Minnesota. In 1828 the fort was an isolated outpost in a territory still settled by Native Americans. Still, the fort was a beehive of activity. Military parades that included more than a hundred men stationed at the fort probably delighted the eldest Taylor girls, Ann, age 17, and Sarah, 14. A stream of officers came through, including Robert Wood, an assistant surgeon who caught Ann's

Fort Snelling, where Taylor served around 1830, sits on a bluff high above the Mississippi River at the edge of present-day Minneapolis and St. Paul, Minnesota. This view was painted nearly 20 years later, and European settlers were still sharing the region with Native Americans.

eye. The two were married in 1829 at Prairie du Chien, down the Mississippi River, in what eventually became Wisconsin. Taylor had been ordered to Fort Crawford in Prairie du Chien. This run-down fort had been damaged by floods, and Taylor's job was to supervise the building of a new fort.

Taylor was a man of regular habits. He went to bed at nine o'clock and rose early. After breakfast he liked to stroll down the banks of the Mississippi. If

Taylor Gives a "Wooling" and Gets Something Worse

Zachary Taylor had a direct, unpretentious manner that made him popular with ordinary soldiers. One story that traveled widely in the army involved Taylor and a German American soldier who didn't understand English very well. One day Taylor was reviewing the troops during a dress parade. The German soldier was out of line and Taylor ordered him to correct his position. When the soldier didn't move, Taylor repeated the order several times. Still, the soldier didn't move.

Believing that the soldier was disobeying him on purpose, Taylor grabbed him by the ears and shook him roughly, an accepted military punishment called "wooling." The surprised soldier reacted by punching Taylor in the jaw, knocking him down. Several officers raised their guns, ready to shoot the soldier for the attack. Taylor realized, however, that the soldier hadn't understood his commands.

He got up quickly and said, "Let the man alone. He will make a good soldier."

☆ ☆ ☆

a steamboat had arrived, he would chat with the captain and passengers. "What's the news from Washington?" he would ask. "How's the Louisville tobacco crop?"

The Black Hawk War

In May 1832, Taylor was ordered to join forces with General Henry Atkinson in northern Illinois, where Black Hawk, the leader of the Sac and Fox people, had returned, hoping to reclaim the tribes' old territory. The Sac and Fox had agreed earlier to give up their land in Illinois and move west across the Mississippi River.

Atkinson planned an attack using his own forces and those commanded by Taylor. Taylor, newly promoted to colonel, was to sail up the Rock River with about 700 men and supplies and meet Atkinson's larger force at a settlement called Dixon's Ferry. Atkinson's troops were undisciplined and poorly trained, however. Instead of marching to Dixon's Ferry, one of the land-based commanders sent a group of men farther north to Black Hawk's encampment to force him to surrender.

The Sac and Fox fighters were poorly supplied. They had little to eat and not much ammunition. Black Hawk realized he was greatly outnumbered and was ready to surrender. He sent three representatives carrying a white flag to the company of soldiers. None of them could understand the Sac language. They ignored the white flag (which means "we surrender") and took two of the three messengers captive. Soon afterward, they killed two Sac fighters who had been sent to observe the surrender.

Indian Removal

Zachary Taylor's struggles against Black Hawk in the Upper Mississippi and later against the Seminole people in Florida were a result of the nation's Indian Removal policy. Thomas Jefferson (president from 1801 to 1809) encouraged American Indians who did not want to adapt to the ways of white communities to move west of the Mississippi. After the War of 1812, the government began signing removal treaties with some tribes in the Old Northwest, including Black Hawk's people. The Native Americans received some payment for their lands and were promised freedom to live west of the Mississippi. In the south, the Cherokee, Chickasaw, Choctaw, Creek, and Seminole people had no interest in moving to Indian Territory, though white settlers pressured them constantly.

In 1830, when former Indian-fighter Andrew Jackson was president, Congress passed the Indian Removal Act, which set aside federal money to move the Indians, by force if necessary. Federal marshals arrived to negotiate removal treaties with the southern tribes, and most of them agreed to go. Some Seminole in Florida, however, chose to fight for their ancestral lands. The most tragic episode in the history of Indian removal was the long trek of the Cherokee people from Georgia and the Carolinas. About 16,000 of them were forcibly moved west to Oklahoma under military guard in the winter of 1838. Cold weather, lack of food and clothing, and disease killed as many as 4,000 along the way, on what became known as the "Trail of Tears."

☆ ★ ☆

When Black Hawk learned that the surrender party was captured and two of his fighters had been killed, he reluctantly gathered his small force and rode toward the U.S. army encampment, expecting to be slaughtered by the larger force. The army recruits, however, were in no mood to fight. When they saw the Sac and Fox warriors, they panicked and ran. A few had horses, but many others ran or walked 25 miles (40 km), all the way to Dixon's Ferry. The Sac and Fox did not follow. Instead, they helped themselves to the food and weapons in the abandoned army camp and went their way.

Disgusted with the troops' behavior, Taylor called their flight "shameful." Black Hawk's attempts to surrender never succeeded, and his "victory" that day soon led to a terrible defeat. Weeks later, the angry soldiers, eager to prove themselves, attacked the poorly supplied Sac and Fox at Bad Axe and killed 150 of them, ending the Black Hawk War. Taylor played a minor role in the battle and later helped to take care of the administrative details that officially brought the war to a close. Then he returned to Fort Crawford.

Jefferson Davis and "Knox" ——————

After the Black Hawk War, Lieutenant Jefferson Davis, who had fought under Taylor, served as his adjutant (or assistant) at Fort Crawford. This brought him in close contact with Taylor's family. In the fall of 1832, the Taylors' daughter Sarah

At the Battle of Bad Axe, retreating Sac and Fox warriors were cut off by U.S. troops. Hundreds were killed or drowned trying to swim across the Mississippi to safety.

Knox, affectionately known as "Knox," was a charming young woman of 18, with a striking head of brown, wavy hair. She admired the young lieutenant's lively intelligence, and the attraction was mutual. Taylor was disturbed by their blossoming romance, however. Although he was devoted to the military life, he didn't want his daughter to marry an army officer. They were away from their families too much. "I know enough of the family life of officers," he told a friend. "I scarcely know my own children or they me."

Taylor forbade the couple to meet, but they managed to see each other on the sly. In June 1835, when Knox was in Louisville visiting her aunt, she and Jefferson Davis were married. Davis had already sent in his resignation from the army to please his father-in-law. While the couple were staying at the plantation

Young Jefferson Davis married the Taylors' daughter Knox, but she died three months later. Davis was a senator from Mississippi when Taylor was president. He later became president of the Confederate States during the Civil War.

of the groom's sister, they both came down with malaria, a fever transmitted from person to person by mosquitoes. Davis eventually recovered, but on September 15, Knox died. Davis was heartbroken. For eight years, he refused to go to parties or dances. He lived quietly on his brother's plantation, managing the huge estate and mourning his beloved wife. Zachary and Peggy Taylor must have mourned Knox's death, too, but they left no record of their grief.

Florida

In 1837 Taylor's 1st Infantry was ordered to Tampa Bay, in Florida Territory, to try to force the remaining Seminole people to leave. The U.S. government wanted them to move to Indian Territory beyond the Mississippi River. Those who refused to leave had hidden themselves in the swampy interior of Florida, frustrating white settlers, the government, and the army.

Taylor pursued a large band of Seminole to the shores of Lake Okeechobee in southern Florida with a force of 1,000 men. His battle plan was simple—to attack the Seminole fighters head-on. About 700 Seminole waited with three chiefs—Sam Jones, Alligator, and Wild Cat. Between the army and the Seminole was a swamp so thick with muddy ooze that horses could not be used, and soldiers had great difficulty crossing it on foot.

Taylor's attack began on Christmas Day 1837. The Missouri volunteers in the front line advanced within 20 yards of the Seminole, who then began firing. The Missourians' leader fell immediately, and they did not re-form their line. Next, five companies of the 6th Infantry pressed forward, and under relentless fire took the heaviest casualties—nearly every one of their officers was killed. The men re-formed and kept up the attack. The Seminole began to run. Finally, Taylor's 1st Infantry entered the fray, and the last of the Seminole fled. In two and a half hours, eleven Seminole and twenty-six soldiers were killed. Taylor's victory was widely reported, and he received a brevet promotion to brigadier general. Alligator and his men finally surrendered in the spring, but 3,000 elusive Seminole remained in Florida. Taylor pursued them for another two years. He was relieved of his assignment in Florida in the spring of 1840.

Before taking up his next post, Taylor and his family did some traveling. They stopped in Philadelphia, where Betty was attending boarding school. In Boston, they arranged for Richard to study with a tutor. Then the couple and Betty traveled west. They visited Niagara Falls and Louisville and finally went home to Baton Rouge.

Taylor welcomed a chance to spend time on his plantations. When he was away, he continued to supervise its affairs from a distance, but he worried about them. As prices for crops changed from year to year, Taylor did not always make a profit in his farming ventures. The few records we have suggest that he did look out for the welfare of his slaves, making sure that they ate well and lived in clean, well-furnished quarters.

Chapter 3

Bound for Texas

Zachary Taylor left Florida at the age of 56 with a reputation in the army as an able commander in the field and an experienced military administrator. If his superiors in the army had any complaints about him, they were that he stubbornly defended his decisions and recommendations and that his blunt, outspoken manner sometimes irritated others. Outside the army, scarcely anyone knew the name Zachary Taylor.

In 1841 Taylor was ordered to Fort Smith, Arkansas, where he took command of the Second Military District, a vast expanse of land that ran from the Mississippi River to the western edge of Indian Territory and from southern Missouri to the Louisiana and Texas borders. There he proved again his talent for administering the army in peaceful but delicate situations. He urged the abandonment of two poorly located forts and supervised construction of a new fort near the western edge of the region. Most important, he worked to preserve peace between the many Native American groups now settled there. He attended large Native American conferences and protected the tribes from attacks by white settlers.

Meanwhile, a major military crisis was approaching. In the 1830s, settlers from the United States began moving into Texas, then a territory of Mexico. In 1836 these settlers declared their independence from Mexico. Mexico tried to put down the Texas rebellion, but failed. The residents of Texas asked the United States to annex the territory, but the U.S. government was slow to act. Some Americans opposed bringing Texas into the United States because it would likely become a large and powerful slave state. Others were opposed because annexation was likely to cause a war with Mexico, which had never recognized the independence of Texas.

Then in March 1845, Congress approved the annexation of Texas, and President John Tyler signed the bill into law. Days later, the newly elected president, James K. Polk, began working toward making Texas a state. In the meantime, Mexico protested the U.S. action and cut all diplomatic ties.

That summer, Polk ordered a military force commanded by Zachary Taylor to set up camp at Corpus Christi, Texas, where the Nueces River flows into the Gulf of Mexico. Among the disagreements between Mexico and the United States was the proper border between Texas and Mexico. The Mexican government held that the border was the Nueces River. Texas and the United States maintained that the border was the Rio Grande, the larger river about 100 miles (160 km) west and south of the Nueces.

An "Army of Occupation" commanded by Taylor stretches as far as the eye can see along the Gulf Coast at Corpus Christi, Texas, late in 1845.

In December Congress voted to make Texas the 28th state. Mexico considered this an act of war. President Polk sent a representative to Mexico to settle the dispute without bloodshed, but his proposal was a daring one. He asked Mexico to accept the Rio Grande as its border with Texas *and* sell its province of Upper California to the United States for $30 million. The Mexicans refused even to speak with Polk's representative.

Polk decided to increase the pressure on Mexico. He ordered Taylor to cross the Nueces River into the disputed territory and to build a fort on the northeast bank of the Rio Grande. In late March of 1846, Taylor began building Fort Texas on the Rio Grande. Meanwhile, thousands of Mexican soldiers began to gather in Matamoros, on the other side of the river. On April 24, the Mexican General Mariano Arista sent about 1,600 men across the Rio Grande, west of Fort Texas. Taylor learned of the river crossing and sent Captain Seth Thornton with two companies of men to find out where the Mexicans were. The next morning Thornton and his men were ambushed about 30 miles (48 km) from Fort Texas. Eleven U.S. soldiers were killed and the remaining 46 were captured.

Taylor immediately reported the skirmish to Washington. Polk received the message on May 9, and two days later he sent a message to Congress requesting a declaration of war against Mexico. After some bitter debate, Congress

In 1846 Taylor marched into territory claimed by both Mexico and Texas. He built Fort Texas (right) on the Rio Grande. Across the river is the town of Matamoros, Mexico.

passed the declaration on May 13. By then, however, Taylor had met and defeated the Mexican army in the disputed territory.

Palo Alto and Resaca de la Palma ——————

Soon after the ambush, Mexican cannons in Matamoros began firing across the Rio Grande at Fort Texas. The Mexican commander sent a message demanding that the Americans surrender. The defenders refused, although there weren't very many of them. Taylor and most of the American forces were at Point Isabel, northeast of Fort Texas, protecting their supplies. On May 7, after learning of the attack, Taylor and his men headed for the fort.

Meanwhile, the Mexican forces had crossed the Rio Grande and were prepared for battle at the settlement of Palo Alto, about 10 miles (16 km) northeast of Fort Texas. Ever the cool and poised general, Taylor stopped his exhausted men less than a mile from the enemy and told them to fill their canteens and rest for an hour. Each of the two commanders got ready for battle in his own way. Taylor slumped sidesaddle on his beloved horse, Old Whitey, chewed and spit tobacco, and chatted with anyone who wandered by. Arista, the Mexican commander, rode along his lines, shouting "Viva la república!" ("Long live the republic!"). Then the two generals got their troops into battle formation.

Taylor was outnumbered, but he knew that his greatest strength was his artillery—especially lighter field guns mounted on wheels, which could be moved and fired rapidly. They had been devised by Major Sam Ringgold, who had also drilled the soldiers until they could fire again every ten seconds. The Mexicans fired a volley from their 80-year-old cannons and were amazed when the U.S. guns returned the fire—again and again and again. The artillery quickly opened up large gaps in the lines of the astonished Mexicans, who had never seen field guns that fired so fast and so accurately.

Overpowered by U.S. artillery, the Mexicans turned to their experienced cavalry, military units mounted on horses. Late in the afternoon, U.S. Captain James Duncan saw the Mexican cavalry heading in the direction of the U.S. supply train. He ordered the artillery to turn and fire at the advancing horsemen, stopping their advance. The dry grasses in the region had caught fire, and clouds of thick smoke drifted over the battlefield. Under the cover of the smoke, Duncan's artillery quickly moved closer to the Mexican troops. When it opened fire, the Mexicans were thrown into panic and withdrew from the field, ending the fighting for the day.

When dawn broke the next morning, the Mexican forces had broken camp and were riding away toward Fort Texas and the Rio Grande. Taylor was

At Palo Alto, in the first major battle of the war, Taylor's troops do battle with the Mexican army as soldiers behind the line tend the wounded and the horses.

delighted with his victory in the first battle of the war, but he was determined to chase his foe and fight again. In the middle of the afternoon, U.S. scouts found them about 5 miles (8 km) away, in a bowl-shaped ravine called the Resaca de la Palma. (A resaca is a dry streambed.) They were protected on all sides by dense, prickly desert bushes called chaparral. The brush made it difficult for the Americans to use their artillery but also handicapped the Mexican cavalry. By late afternoon, the two armies were fighting hand-to-hand. Only the Mexican cannons, in place before the battle, could fire effectively. Taylor shouted at Colonel William Belknap, "Take those guns and by God, keep them!" Belknap's two infantry units obeyed, charging down the brush-filled slope and seizing the battery. When the cannons fell silent, Mexican forces began to panic. Many of Arista's soldiers gave up the fight and began running toward the Rio Grande. Taylor had won his second victory in two days. Ten days later, he crossed the Rio Grande and captured the Mexican town of Matamoros.

The Mexican army lost 256 soldiers in battle, compared with 58 for the Americans. Many more Mexicans deserted or were drowned trying to swim across the Rio Grande. Although outnumbered, Taylor's forces had used their rapid-fire artillery at Palo Alto and had proved that they could fight hand-to-hand under difficult conditions at Resaca de la Palma. The U.S. troops now controlled the lower Rio Grande Valley and all the disputed territory.

Fast Facts

THE U.S.- MEXICAN WAR

Who: The United States and Mexico

When: The U.S. Congress declared war against Mexico on May 13, 1846. Fighting ended in September 1847. The Treaty of Guadalupe Hidalgo was signed on February 2, 1848.

Why: When the U.S. made Texas, a former territory of Mexico, a state in 1845, Mexico threatened war. U.S. troops entered territory claimed by both nations in 1846 and were attacked by Mexican forces in April 1846.

Where: The U.S. drove Mexican forces out of Texas and captured Monterrey in northern Mexico. They also captured parts of present-day New Mexico and California. In early 1847, a U.S. force landed at Veracruz, on Mexico's Gulf coast, and fought its way to Mexico City. The Mexican capital was occupied in September, ending the major fighting.

Outcome: In the Treaty of Guadalupe Hidalgo, Mexico ceded more than 500,000 square miles (1.3 million km^2) to the U.S., including all or most of present-day California, Nevada, Arizona, Utah, and New Mexico and parts of five other states. The U.S. paid Mexico $15 million and all claims of U.S. citizens against Mexico.

When news of the battles reached the rest of the United States, Taylor became a celebrity. Writer and poet Walt Whitman compared Taylor to George Washington. "Our Commander on the Rio Grande," he said, "emulates the Great Commander of our revolution." Stories of Taylor's bravery were greatly exaggerated. One tall tale claimed that while mounted on Old Whitey, he could measure the speed of an oncoming artillery ball and rise in his saddle at just the right moment to allow the ball to pass between him and his horse. President Polk probably didn't believe that tale, but he did send Taylor a letter of congratulation and promoted him to brevet major general. The next month, Taylor received the full rank of major general.

By the fall of 1846, Taylor's army had swelled to about 7,000 men, many of them fresh volunteers who had signed up for duty after Congress declared war. He received orders from Washington to attack the town of Monterrey, east of Matamoros at the foot of the mountains called the Sierra Madre. After a hard three-day battle against the army of General Pedro de Ampudia, Taylor's forces captured the city on September 23, 1846. After General Ampudia surrendered, Taylor agreed to Ampudia's request for an eight-week armistice during which there would be no fighting. For the Americans, the battle of Monterrey was the costliest yet: 122 men were killed and 368 were wounded.

Taylor sent a messenger to Washington with the good news of the fall of Monterrey. The commander awaited Polk's congratulations, but he never received them. The president was angry that Taylor had agreed to a long armistice. He believed that if Taylor had pursued the Mexican army, Mexico might have surrendered and ended the war. In the United States, more and more people were expressing doubts about the war, and Polk was eager to finish it. He decided to order his most senior general, Winfield Scott, to mount an aggressive attack on Mexico City, the nation's capital, far to the south.

Taylor learned of President Polk's plan in November. He was asked to send half of his army to join General Scott's force and to hold northern Mexico with his remaining men. Taylor was disappointed. Even though he had achieved a series of major victories, he would take no part in the new campaign. His pride wounded, he grumbled to his son-in-law, "I [have] been stripped of nearly the whole of the regular force, & more than one half of the volunteers."

In early January 1847, the U.S. plans for an invasion of southern Mexico fell into the hands of the Mexican president and general, Antonio López de Santa Anna. When he saw that Taylor would be trying to hold northern Mexico with a very small force, he realized that he had a chance to destroy Taylor's army at Monterrey, then hurry south to defend Mexico City against General Scott's invaders. It was his best chance to win the war.

On Sunday, February 21, Taylor learned that Santa Anna's army was approaching Monterrey. He understood that Santa Anna had nearly 20,000 troops to attack his own army of only 5,000. He quickly moved his forces to a mountain pass southwest of Monterrey near the Hacienda de Buena Vista, a large estate. Surrounded by towering peaks, the pass offered the outnumbered Americans a good defensive position. Santa Anna arrived at 11 o'clock Monday morning and sent Taylor a formal request for surrender, warning him that he was greatly outnumbered. The U.S. general did not scare easily, and he flatly refused.

The battle began in earnest on Tuesday. Santa Anna's strategy was to mass his troops and attack Taylor's defenses at a single point, hoping to overrun and destroy the army. Taylor watched as the Mexican army gathered. As they struggled to get into battle order, Taylor had time to bring field artillery and reinforce-

At Buena Vista, outnumbered nearly four to one, Taylor took the high ground and defended it against Mexican attacks from different directions. The peaks of the Sierra Madre are in the background.

ments from other fronts. He moved fearlessly around the battlefield, encouraging his men to give their all, even under heavy fire.

By dusk the Mexicans were spent, and the Americans still held their positions. The troops prepared for another day of desperate fighting, then wearily tried to sleep. The next morning, they were overjoyed to discover that Santa Anna and his men were retreating. The dead and wounded on the battlefield explained why the Mexicans were on the march. Santa Anna's force had suffered nearly 600 men killed and nearly 3,000 wounded or missing. The U.S. forces suffered 280 killed and nearly 500 wounded or missing.

This desperate battle against a much larger force—and the surprising victory—made Taylor the biggest hero of the U.S.-Mexican War. He would take no part in the final campaign to capture Mexico City, but at home, Americans celebrated Buena Vista as the most courageous and inspiring battle of the conflict. Once again, "Old Rough and Ready" had proved his skill at commanding an army in battle.

One of the soldiers who was killed at Buena Vista was the son of the great U.S. senator Henry Clay. Taylor wrote to Clay, "To your son I felt bound by the strongest ties of private regard; and when I miss his familiar face . . . I can say with truth, that I feel no exultation in our success." Taylor had no idea that he and Clay would soon become opponents on the stage of national politics.

Winfield Scott, General of the Army, who commanded the U.S. expedition that landed on Mexico's Gulf Coast and fought its way to Mexico City. A stickler for detail, he was known as "Old Fuss and Feathers."

Soon after Taylor's victory, General Winfield Scott and his forces landed near Veracruz, on Mexico's Gulf Coast. By the end of March, he had captured the city. In April he began his march inland toward Mexico City. In May he captured Puebla, halfway to the capital. Beginning the final assault in August, he and his troops captured the fort at Chapultepec on September 13 and marched into Mexico City the next day. The surrender of the city ended the major fighting, but a peace treaty would not be signed until February 1848.

In the meantime, Taylor and his forces continued to patrol northern Mexico. He realized that he would see no more combat in the war and became impatient to go home. "I will not remain longer in this country than duty and honor compel me," he wrote to his daughter Ann.

Chapter 4

The Hero Returns —————————————

Taylor returned to the United States in December 1847 to a hero's welcome. In New Orleans, nearly 40,000 people lined the streets to greet the hero of Buena Vista. Taylor rode in procession on Old Whitey, and cannons thundered. (Old Whitey lost more than one hair from his tail to souvenir seekers!) After two days of festivities, the general traveled up the Mississippi River to the quiet of his plantation home in Baton Rouge. He was certainly not forgotten, however. Verses about him appeared in newspapers and magazines. People danced to the "Rough and Ready Polka" and tapped their feet to "General Taylor's Gallop."

The greatest tribute to Taylor was the growing movement to make him the next president of the United States. After his early victories at Palo Alto and Monterrey, a group of Whig congressmen had

Prints like this one showing Taylor as a dashing leader helped make him a popular presidential candidate.

already decided that Taylor would be an appealing candidate. One of those congressmen was Abraham Lincoln from Illinois. After the Battle of Buena Vista, the general's popularity soared. Many Whig politicians and newspaper editors joined the chorus urging him to run. Southern Whigs became Taylor's most enthusiastic supporters. Because Taylor owned a southern plantation and slaves, they thought that Taylor would defend their interests well.

The Slavery Question

Slavery was becoming the single biggest issue in the United States. The end of the U.S.-Mexican War and the addition of huge new territories to the country only focused attention more strongly on the slavery question.

Even during the war, U.S. senators and representatives had been trying to reach an agreement about whether slavery would be permitted in any new lands acquired from Mexico. Most southern congressmen thought it should be allowed; most northerners opposed it. On August 8, 1846, the House of Representatives was debating a bill appropriating money for the war. David Wilmot, a representative from Pennsylvania, proposed an amendment to the bill stating that slavery would be prohibited in any territory acquired from Mexico as a result of the war. The amendment, known as the Wilmot Proviso, eventually passed the House after

Many Views on Slavery

The slavery debate was very complicated. Only a few Americans held extreme views. In the South, a group sometimes called the *fire-eaters* defended slavery as moral and acceptable everywhere. In the North, the *abolitionists* believed that slavery was morally wrong and should be ended as soon as possible throughout the country. A few extremists on both sides believed that violence should be used if peaceful means failed.

Most people held views somewhere between these extremes. Some were mostly concerned about economic issues. Southerners were prospering because of strong demand for cotton, and they needed slaves to continue producing it. They believed that those against slavery wanted to destroy their economy. Many settlers in the new western territories were farmers who cleared land and raised crops with their own hands. They were afraid that if slavery were permitted there, large plantation owners could push them aside, using cheaper slave labor. These settlers were for "free soil," and were against the spread of slavery to their region.

Political leaders were worried about the balance of power in Congress. Southerners were determined to keep the number of free and slave states even so that they would be able to control the Senate, in which each state has two senators. Because the North had a larger population, it already had a strong majority in the House of Representatives, where states with large populations have more representatives than those with small populations. Southerners believed that if they were outnumbered in both houses of Congress, northerners would pass laws damaging to the South.

Political leaders like Henry Clay were seeking a compromise that moderates in the North and South could agree on to reduce suspicion and rivalry between regions and keep the country together.

a heated debate. In the Senate, the proviso was opposed by southern senators and was eventually defeated, so it never took effect.

Even though it never became law, the Wilmot Proviso focused attention on the issue of slavery in the new territories. President Polk opposed the proviso, but many antislavery Democrats supported it. The Whig party was also divided between proslavery and antislavery supporters. The issue would be on the minds of many voters during the presidential election of 1848.

The Whigs Choose Taylor

The Democrats held their national nominating convention in Baltimore on May 22 to 25, 1848, and nominated Lewis Cass on the fourth ballot. Cass was a northerner who had served in a wide variety of government posts—governor of the Michigan Territory, secretary of war, minister to France, and senator from Michigan. Cass, like President Polk, opposed the Wilmot Proviso and favored "popular sovereignty," allowing people in each territory to decide for themselves whether slavery would be permitted. To strengthen their ticket, the Democrats chose a military man for vice president—General William Butler of Kentucky.

Two weeks later, the Whigs gathered in Philadelphia. Taylor's supporters met all the trains bringing convention delegates and promoted Taylor's candidacy

This Whig campaign banner shows Taylor and vice-presidential candidate Millard Fillmore surrounded by patriotic images.

A Convention for Women

All the people who attended the Democratic and Whig conventions in 1848 were men. The reason for that was simple—women were not allowed to vote or run for office. That summer, however, there was another important political convention, and it was organized to try to change the situation.

On July 19, about 200 women and 40 men gathered in Seneca Falls, New York, to attend the first convention on women's rights. The organizers presented a declaration based on the Declaration of Independence. It said, "We hold these truths to be self evident: that all men *and women* are created equal." Speakers urged that laws restricting women from owning property and holding jobs be changed, that women receive increased educational opportunities, and that they be given the right to vote.

Most newspapers and magazines made fun of the convention. The ideas that women should be able to own property, work for pay, and vote were revolutionary. After 1848 women's conventions were held every year, and they slowly changed the nation's thinking and its laws. It took 72 years, until 1920, for women to gain the right to vote in federal elections.

☆ ☆ ☆

with signs, campaign pins, music, and lots of talk. As the Whigs crowded the city, Taylor supporters were everywhere. One man described the lively scene: "Streets were thronged—Chestnut Street especially was almost walled up with men; and all seemed mad with excitement on politics—such gesticulating and jabbering you never saw or heard."

The Whig convention began on June 7. Taylor's main rival for the presidential nomination was Henry Clay. Now 70 years old, Clay had been a leading political voice for more than 30 years, serving as speaker of the House of Representatives and senator from Kentucky and becoming a founder of the Whig party. He had run twice before for the presidency, in 1832 and 1844. Clay had many friends and strong support, but he also had many enemies. Another candidate was General Winfield Scott, the hero of the march to Mexico City.

By the third ballot, it became clear that Taylor was going to win. His supporters stood on chairs and cheered until they were hoarse. On the fourth ballot, many Clay supporters switched to Taylor, and he won. Southern Whigs had given "Old Zach" most of his votes. To attract northern voters, the party nominated Millard Fillmore from New York for vice president. Taylor and Fillmore made an interesting contrast. Taylor came from a prosperous and prominent southern family, while Fillmore was born into a very poor family. Yet Taylor dressed carelessly and looked undistinguished, while Fillmore dressed stylishly and seemed more "presidential."

It was clear that the main issue dividing the country was slavery. The issue was so emotional, however, that both Whigs and Democrats decided to say as little about it as possible. A candidate might win half the voters by coming out for or against slavery, but he was sure to lose the other half. Both parties were split on the issue, so they united behind their candidates and left the slavery question unmentioned.

For a few leaders in both parties, this silence was too much. Deeply opposed to the spread of slavery, they gave up their commitment to the Whig or Democratic party and formed a new party instead. In the second week of August, more than 10,000 of them gathered under a huge tent in Buffalo, New York. They

Like other candidates in 1848, Taylor was reluctant to say anything specific about the emotional issues dividing the country. This cartoon makes fun of his silence.

called themselves the Free Soil party, and they enthusiastically nominated former Democratic president Martin Van Buren to be their candidate for president. Unlike the Democrats and Whigs, the Free Soilers made slavery the most important issue of their campaign. They supported the Wilmot Proviso, which proposed to outlaw slavery in the new lands gained from Mexico.

Van Buren's nomination was bad news for Democratic candidate Lewis Cass. Van Buren was popular and still powerful in New York State, and he vowed to defeat Cass in his home state. Democrats worried that if Cass lost New York (which had the largest population and the most electoral votes of any state), he might lose the election.

The Election of 1848

Following the practice of the time, Taylor did not campaign actively for himself. He spent the summer working at his Baton Rouge army headquarters and looking after his cotton crops. The Whig campaign leaders didn't explain Taylor's political views or his legislative plans. Instead, they praised his leadership skills and his glorious victories in the U.S.-Mexican War. They also heaped scorn on the Democrats and their candidates.

During the last two months of the campaign, Senator John Crittenden, an old friend of Taylor's and a fellow Kentuckian, took charge of the campaign. Like

This cartoon shows Taylor on a throne of human skulls, reminding voters that Taylor's main claim to fame as an army commander was his effectiveness in killing.

an army general, he sent out speakers where they were needed. Abraham Lincoln spoke in Illinois and Massachusetts. William Seward, the forceful antislavery politician from New York, spoke to northern audiences in New York and Ohio. "We shall have a most overwhelming, glorious triumph," Abraham Lincoln wrote as the election approached.

On November 7, 1848, the entire nation went to the polls on the same day for the first time in history. It elected Zachary Taylor, the hero of Buena Vista, with 1,360,099 votes to 1,220,544 for Lewis Cass and 291,263 for Martin Van Buren. Taylor won 163 electoral votes, Cass 127, and Van Buren 0. The crucial state, as Democrats had feared, was New York, where Martin Van Buren won just enough Democratic votes to keep Lewis Cass from winning the state. Taylor won New York's electoral votes, which helped him win election as president.

Soon after the election, the president-elect attended the wedding of his youngest daughter, Betty, to his principal aide, Colonel William Bliss. Betty was a charming 24-year-old who would soon serve as hostess at the White House. In early February, the general said a fond good-bye to his neighbors and friends in Baton Rouge and headed for Washington. He arrived on February 23. Blazing bonfires, roaring guns, and a large crowd greeted him as he made his way from the train station to his rooms at the Willard Hotel.

Chapter 5

Taylor Takes Office

Thousands of visitors poured into the nation's capital on March 5, 1849, to see Zachary Taylor inaugurated as the twelfth president of the United States. Fashionably dressed New Yorkers and rough-looking frontier folk lined Pennsylvania Avenue and cheered as Taylor's horse-drawn carriage drove by on its way to the Capitol. The president-elect tipped his hat to acknowledge the enthusiastic crowd. He looked a bit like an old frontiersman himself, with his heavy, muscular face, weather-beaten skin, and coarse, thinning hair.

Under a cloudy sky, Taylor delivered his inaugural address outside the Capitol building before a crowd of about 20,000 people. It was one of the shortest in history. He did not say how he wanted to settle the burning issue of the day—the extension of slavery into the new territories. For those who were listening carefully, though, there was a hint that the president's priority might be the preservation of the Union. He assured his audience, "My Administration [will] be devoted to the welfare of the whole country, and not to the support of any particular section."

An artist's version of Taylor's inauguration with portraits of many political leaders.

Nathaniel Hawthorne Loses His Job

When Zachary Taylor became president, he followed the practice of previous presidents and asked for the resignation of many Democratic officeholders to make way for loyal Whigs. One Democrat who lost his job was Nathaniel Hawthorne, a writer who had a position at the federal customs office in Salem, Massachusetts. Hawthorne was upset about losing the job, but used his new free time well. He completed his novel *The Scarlet Letter*, then wrote another, *The House of Seven Gables*. The two works are among the great classics in American literature.

☆ ☆ ☆

By the time the Taylors and Fillmores drove through the rutted streets of Washington to attend the glittering inaugural balls, it was snowing. One of the managers of these all-night celebrations was Abraham Lincoln. At four in the morning, Lincoln could not find his hat under the chest-high pile of coats in the cloakroom and walked home in the snow without it!

Taylor was careful to balance his cabinet with members from the North and the South. The politically inexperienced president soon became friends with another new face in Washington, William Seward. The powerful antislavery Whig from New York had just been elected senator, and he became one of Taylor's closest advisers. After he had met Taylor for the first, time Seward wrote, "He is the most gentle-looking and amiable of men. Every word and look indicate sincerity of heart." When Seward, known for his strong views against slavery, began attending cabinet meetings, many southerners grew nervous.

William Seward, senator from New York, became a friend and adviser to President Taylor. He later served in Abraham Lincoln's cabinet and negotiated the purchase of Alaska from Russia.

Trouble in Nicaragua

Less than two weeks after his inauguration, Taylor received a troubling report from a U.S. diplomat in Central America. Nicaragua, Honduras, and El Salvador were protesting the British invasion of San Juan, a Nicaraguan town on the shore of the Caribbean Sea. San Juan was the point at which Great Britain hoped one day to dig a canal from the Caribbean to the Pacific Ocean. Such a canal would make it easier for ships to reach the Pacific. Without a canal, ships had to sail all the way around South America, crossing the dangerous Strait of Magellan at the tip of the continent. A Nicaraguan canal would reduce the trip by thousands of miles. The British had gained control of San Juan indirectly. They crowned a local Native American leader and declared that he would rule under British protection.

This report troubled Taylor. Since the presidency of James Monroe, the United States had warned European nations against meddling in the affairs of countries in the Americas. Also, the United States was very interested in digging a canal that would connect the Atlantic and the Pacific Oceans. Now that California and the Oregon Territory were part of the United States, there was an increased need for a shorter route between the oceans.

Taylor asked his secretary of state, John Clayton, to begin discussions with Great Britain. After months of difficult negotiations, the two nations signed the Clayton-Bulwer Treaty in April 1850. According to the treaty, neither country would have exclusive control over a canal or try to establish new colonies in Central America.

Crisis on the Home Front ———————————

The Nicaragua issue was a small matter compared to the issues at home. In February of 1848, gold had been discovered in California. As the news spread, thousands of prospectors were in a race to reach California, hoping to strike it rich in the goldfields. The region badly needed a civilian government to replace the military government then in operation. Again, the question arose—would slavery be permitted in the territory or not?

Taylor devised a simple but clever plan. If California became an official territory, the usual step before statehood, Congress would have to decide whether slavery would be permitted there. This would result in a long, angry debate between the North and the South. To avoid this, Taylor planned to encourage California to apply for statehood immediately. It would draw up a state constitution, which could declare whether slavery would be permitted. Taylor was confident that Californians would not allow slavery, and that was fine with him. He thought Congress would respect the stated wishes of California's residents.

In April 1849, Taylor quietly sent Thomas Butler King, a Georgia congressman, to California to promote his plan. By November leaders of the region

The States During the Presidency of Zachary Taylor

ORIGINAL STATES

As gold fever spread in the east, people looked for ways to get to California. Many simply walked 2,000 miles or more, carrying their possessions on pack animals or in wagons (above). Those who could afford it chose passage on ships, which traveled 9,000 miles around the tip of South America (right).

had drafted a state constitution that outlawed slavery. Of course, their application for statehood would still need the approval of Congress.

While Californians were drawing up their constitution, the president faced another problem. For more than a decade, Texas had claimed that Santa Fe County in New Mexico was part of Texas. The Santa Fe region had its own history and interests. The residents of the county did not want to be part of Texas, partly because Texas had become a slave state. They hoped to become part of a new territory to be called New Mexico. Taylor had another plan, however. He quietly sent a deputy to the region to suggest that it apply for statehood, just as California was doing. When New Mexico was admitted as a free state, the nation's courts could decide the claims of Texas to the Santa Fe region.

In his annual report to Congress on December 4, 1849, Taylor openly stated his policies about the lands won from Mexico. He recommended that California be granted statehood and that its desire to be free, rather than slave, be respected. He predicted that New Mexico would apply for statehood in the near future under the same terms, and he urged Congress to welcome it into the Union. Taylor was urging Congress to take a middle course on the slavery issue, leaving open the possibility that a new state may or may not permit it. He concluded his report with a clear statement of his own beliefs, describing the danger he saw and the position he would take:

In my opinion [the] dissolution [of the Union] would be the greatest of

calamities, and to avert that should be the study of every American.

Upon its preservation must depend our happiness and that of countless

generations to come. Whatever dangers may threaten it, I shall stand by

it and maintain it in its integrity to the full extent of the obligations

imposed and the powers conferred upon me by the Constitution.

During the difficult months that he had been in office, Taylor's family and friends gave him a welcome escape from his cares. He had spent much of his life separated from Peggy, his children, and other close relatives and friends. Now he was surrounded by them. Peggy was with him in the White House, of course. Their daughter Betty served as the White House hostess. Her husband, William Bliss, was a brilliant graduate of the U.S. Military Academy. He had served as Zachary Taylor's close assistant and friend since 1842 and became his private secretary in the White House. The Taylors' other daughter, Ann, lived in nearby Baltimore with her husband, who had been one of Taylor's favorite correspondents when he was in Mexico. Their former son-in-law, Jefferson Davis, now remarried, was serving as a senator from Mississippi, and he often visited the White House. Even Old Whitey was around. When Taylor looked out the window in fair weather, he could see his horse grazing peacefully on the lawn.

Zachary Taylor with his daughter's husband, William Bliss. He had served under Taylor in the army and became his private secretary in the White House.

On January 1, Taylor and his family welcomed thousands to the White House for a traditional reception. For two hours, a stream of guests poured in— foreign diplomats, justices of the Supreme Court, congressmen, and ordinary folk. William Seward brought his children, who probably enjoyed listening to the Marine Band. Other visitors admired the new drapes and china in the freshly decorated East Room. On that day, at least, the people of the United States could unite in the common goal of ringing in a New Year.

The Congress of 1850

All the Christmas and New Year's cheer seemed to evaporate within weeks. Many southerners were furious with Taylor, who they believed had betrayed them. They had trusted Taylor as a fellow slaveholder to defend their region and the preservation of slavery. They were shocked to learn that he seemed to oppose the spread of slavery into the new territories. Before the election, they had never asked him to clarify his beliefs on the issue, and as one historian put it, they had played an incredible trick on themselves.

In January, the senators argued heatedly over what to do with California's application for statehood. They also debated the best response to the border dispute between New Mexico and Texas and to New Mexico's expected application for statehood. In addition, southern slaveholders were complaining that northern governments refused to return fugitive (runaway) slaves, as the law required. Antislavery forces were upset about the practice of slavery in the nation's capital. Only seven blocks away from the Capitol building was a warehouse that belonged to the largest slave trader in the country.

As Congress struggled to bring all these emotional issues into perspective, the Senate chamber became a stage for three great statesmen who seemed to tower

majestically over the younger senators. Daniel Webster from Massachusetts was the Senate's greatest orator. Now 68 years old, he had grown increasingly opposed to slavery. John C. Calhoun of South Carolina was the most powerful supporter of states' rights and the claims of the South. Also 68 years old, he was desperately ill with tuberculosis. The third giant was Henry Clay, now 73, who represented Kentucky. In his long career, he had worked out many difficult compromises in Congress and had run for president on a major-party ticket three times.

Henry Clay, the Great Compromiser, who drafted the Missouri Compromise and ran for president three times. The compromise he proposed in 1850 led to a bitter feud with President Taylor.

On February 5, a clear and wintry day, Clay presented a new compromise plan to a packed Senate. Word had gotten out that he was going to give a historic speech, and the galleries were crowded with diplomats, politicians, and fashionably dressed women. Clay spoke for three hours, and then for almost two more hours the next day. He urged that California be admitted as a state and be allowed to choose whether to permit slavery, which was very close to Taylor's position. He recommended that New Mexico and other territories won from Mexico be organized into territorial governments with no decision on slavery. He argued that Texas must drop its claim to Santa Fe County, New Mexico. To appeal to anti-slavery voters, he proposed that the slave trade (but not slavery) be outlawed in Washington, D.C. Finally, to appeal to southerners, he urged a stricter fugitive slave law, requiring northern states to track down and return runaway slaves to their owners. Clay urged his listeners to adopt a spirit of compromise or face the "irretrievable destruction" of the Union.

Taylor did not comment publicly on Clay's plan, but a week later he forwarded to Congress a copy of the California state constitution, which prohibited slavery, for its approval.

On March 4, John C. Calhoun rose to his feet on the Senate floor. He was too weak to deliver his speech and asked another senator to read it to a hushed

John C. Calhoun, critically ill with tuberculosis, asked another senator to read his fiery speech condemning Clay's compromise.

crowd that overflowed the Senate chamber. Calhoun's address criticized President Taylor's plan and accused him of manipulating California voters to request the status of a free state. He also criticized Clay's plan, saying that it did not restore a necessary balance of power between North and South. The darkest passage in Calhoun's speech concerned the possibility that states might secede—withdraw from the United States altogether. He said, "It is a great mistake to suppose that disunion can be effected at a single blow. The cords which bind these states together in one common Union are far too numerous and powerful for that. . . . Already the agitation of the slavery question has snapped some of the most important [cords], and has greatly weakened all the others."

A few days later Daniel Webster was the last of the three great senators to speak. Again, the Senate galleries were filled. He was known to sympathize with the views of the Free Soil party, and many expected a speech against slavery in the territories. Instead, as one historian put it, Webster bowed his head to the storm and made a plea for the Union. "I do speak today," he said, "not as a Massachusetts man, nor as a Northern man, but as an American. I speak for the preservation of the Union." He begged his fellow senators to be more tolerant and admitted that the South had some legitimate complaints. The next day, he told a friend that he had forgotten to compliment the president on his plan and to say that he would vote for it.

Daniel Webster was a powerful opponent of slavery, but he urged the Senate to vote for Clay's compromise, including the Fugitive Slave Act, to keep the Union from breaking apart.

After the giants had spoken, others chimed in. Jefferson Davis, President Taylor's old friend, now plantation owner in Mississippi, wanted slavery permitted in New Mexico. William Seward of New York, Taylor's friend and ally, spoke passionately against slavery, angering many moderates, including the president.

In mid-March some southern senators suggested that Henry Clay's proposals be combined into a single "omnibus" bill that could be voted on as a package, rather than as separate measures. Clay agreed, but many others objected. President Taylor was angry that Henry Clay had put the president's plan on the sidelines. Taylor believed his own plan should be passed. He also thought that the

An artist's view of the fight in the Senate makes it seem like slapstick comedy.

Congress was reminded on April 17 how hot tempers were running. A fiery southern senator, Henry Foote, was condemning and ridiculing Senator Thomas Hart Benton, who sympathized with Free Soil ideas. It was not the first time Foote had done this. On this day, Benton lost his patience, left his chair, and approached Foote. Foote drew a pistol and pointed it at Benton.

"I have no pistols!" Benton yelled. "Let him fire! Stand out of the way! Let the assassin fire!"

The men were quickly separated, but no one in the chamber would forget their dramatic exchange.

★ ☆ ☆

omnibus bill would never pass in Congress because there was too much disagreement on each proposal.

In early May, Clay presented his committee's omnibus bill, and debates on the bill began. Some senators, loyal to the president and his plan, hesitated to support Clay's bill and remained silent. Clay had never openly criticized the president's plan, but finally he spoke, comparing Taylor's plan to his own. The president's plan addressed only the problem of California, he argued. The omnibus plan would also solve the issues of a government for New Mexico, that region's territorial disagreement with Texas, the need for a stronger fugitive slave law, and the issue of slavery in Washington. "Here are five wounds . . . bleeding and threatening the well-being, if not the existence of the body politic," he said. The president's plan, Clay said, would heal only one wound and allow the others to bleed heavily.

Angered and wounded by Clay's words, Taylor attacked him in a newspaper editorial, accusing him of being motivated by a desire for personal glory rather than the good of the nation. The president had many defenders, most of them northern Whigs. Thurlow Weed, a powerful New York Whig and newspaper editor, compared Taylor to the captain of a boat on a stormy sea. "General Taylor," he wrote, "with good Mates and a hearty Crew can take the ship through . . . in safety."

A photograph of President Taylor taken by pioneer photographer Mathew Brady.

Many moderates, however, thought the president's stubbornness, while useful on a battlefield, was not helpful in negotiating with Congress. They were also worried that the dispute between Texas and New Mexico was out of control. By June the draft of a state constitution from New Mexico, forbidding slavery, was on its way to Washington for approval. Meanwhile, Texas was threatening to send soldiers to take possession of Santa Fe County. Taylor was outraged at the threats, even proposing to go there himself. "I will be there before those people shall . . . have a foot of that territory. The whole business is infamous and must be put down," he declared.

The Fourth of July

The arguments in Congress over Clay's compromise bill continued into the summer. On the Fourth of July, Congress and the president took a holiday to celebrate the 74th anniversary of the Declaration of Independence. On that hot, humid day, Taylor attended a ceremony to lay the cornerstone of the unfinished Washington Monument. Henry Foote, the pistol-wielding southern senator, was among the speakers. The president was amazed to hear him urging his listeners to forget about their regional prejudices and rage. He saw Foote after the speech and asked, "Why will you not always speak this way?"

After two hours under the broiling sun, Taylor walked along the Potomac River and returned to the White House in the late afternoon. By then he may have been suffering from sunstroke, and he ate a lot of fruit and drank some cold milk. Hours later, he was seriously ill with powerful stomach cramps. Whether from the heat or from the fruit and milk, his digestive system was inflamed, and he was in agony, showing signs of acute gastroenteritis, an inflammation of the lining of the stomach and intestines. On Friday he felt well enough to sign the final version of the Clayton-Bulwer Treaty, the agreement the United States had reached with Great Britain to settle their dispute over Nicaragua. The next day, the president still felt sick. Doctors at that time did not understand digestive illnesses very well. Taylor's doctor prescribed opium, a narcotic that helps relax the intestines, and calomel, a medication that contains mercury.

In spite of the doctors' efforts, Taylor continued to get worse. On Tuesday, July 9, he said to his doctors, "You have fought a good fight but you cannot make a good stand." Word had gotten around Washington by then that the president was seriously, perhaps fatally, ill.

In the Senate, a southern senator had been boring his listeners for an hour with a proslavery speech when Daniel Webster asked permission to interrupt. "I have a sorrowful message to deliver," he said in an emotional voice. "A great misfortune threatens the nation. The President of the United States, General Taylor, is dying and may not survive the day."

Jefferson Davis rushed to the White House, where Peggy, Taylor's daughters, Ann and Betty, and their husbands were gathered. At about 10 o'clock that evening, the president called his wife to his bedside. He begged her not to cry for him. Then, a true soldier to the end, he said, "I am about to die. I expect the summons soon. I have always endeavored to discharge all my official duties faithfully. I regret nothing, but am sorry that I am about to leave my friends." He died half an hour later.

A grand memorial procession for Zachary Taylor in New York City two weeks after his death.

On Saturday about 100,000 people lined the route to see the funeral procession, which was 2 miles (3 km) long, and to pay their respects. General Winfield Scott, in a sparkling dress uniform and a helmet with a tall plume of yellow feathers, rode with the military escort. The hearse, pulled by eight white horses, was followed by Old Whitey, without a rider and with its stirrups reversed. Then came the carriages with the family, congressmen, and other dignitaries. The president was buried in the Taylor family cemetery outside Louisville, Kentucky, where he had spent his childhood. It is now a national military cemetery.

Chapter 6

A Brief Presidency ————————————

Zachary Taylor was in office for only sixteen months, not long enough for a president to leave a great legacy. The presidency is like no other job, and during the first year in office, every president is inexperienced. Taylor, in particular, had a lot to learn because he had never held any political office and was not familiar with the workings of the federal government. A good president learns from experience, and Taylor's biographers agree that he was improving and gaining confidence with time. It is impossible to predict what he could have accomplished if he had remained in office for his full term.

After his death, Senator Thomas Hart Benton commented sadly on the nation's loss: "His death was a public calamity. No man could have been more devoted to the Union, or more opposed to the slavery agitation; and his position as a Southern man . . . would have

Zachary Taylor in uniform with his horse Old Whitey against a background of battle.

given him a power in the settlement of those questions which no President without these qualifications could have possessed."

Another supporter, Abraham Lincoln, agreed that Taylor's dedication to the Union, rather than to the interests of his southern roots, was one of his finest qualities, and one of the most unexpected.

Historians are not in complete agreement about whether Taylor was right to block Henry Clay's omnibus bill, a measure that was eventually approved in

The President Returns from His Grave

In 1991 a writer who was doing research on Zachary Taylor claimed that he did not die of inflammation of the digestive tract. She was convinced that he had been murdered, and some other historians believed she might be right. The writer thought Taylor was poisoned with arsenic by southern slavery supporters who were angered by the president's policies. Others suspected two antislavery men, Henry Clay and Vice President Millard Fillmore. The two men wanted Clay's compromise bill to pass, and saw Taylor as an obstacle.

With the encouragement of President Taylor's great-great-great grandson, Dabney Taylor, researchers uncovered the president's remains. A national laboratory tested samples of Taylor's hair and bones for arsenic, and the medical examiner of Kentucky concluded that Taylor had not been poisoned. Many people were relieved, including Dabney Taylor. "Rumors have been running through the family for years," he said.

☆ ★ ☆

the form of the Compromise of 1850. Some believe that if Taylor had insisted on his stronger position against extending slavery into the new territories, he might have ended the nation's crisis over the issue. The Compromise of 1850 did not resolve the basic issues, and the result, some ten years later, was the Civil War. Other historians argue that Taylor's plan would not have discouraged southerners from leaving the Union. They simply would have left earlier, and war would have come sooner. These critics believe that the Compromise of 1850 gave the Union ten necessary years in which to grow stronger before the coming of the Civil War.

Taylor's one lasting contribution was in foreign affairs. With his secretary of state, he helped negotiate and finally signed the Clayton-Bulwer Treaty with Britain, which not only ended the dispute about Nicaragua but also helped create an atmosphere in which Great Britain and the United States could finally establish a friendship.

It is a sad irony that scholars have very few papers from Taylor's presidency, because they would have helped to evaluate his administration. His papers were stored in the Louisiana home of his son, Richard, which was burned down by Union forces during the Civil War. (Richard Taylor was unharmed.)

Taylor was one of the least prepared presidents ever elected to the position, with no experience in local, state, or federal office. His military training and sense of command were his greatest strengths and his greatest weaknesses. He inspired confidence in voters and in many political leaders, and seemed genuinely concerned about the country's future welfare. His military experience was a weakness because he was accustomed to delivering orders and to having them obeyed, not to negotiating. In his dealings with Congress, he seemed unable to form alliances with like-minded legislators that might have allowed him to influence the course of the hugely important legislation they were considering.

After Zachary Taylor

Vice President Millard Fillmore was sworn in as president soon after Taylor's death. Fillmore favored Henry Clay's compromise, and as president he would help see it passed and would sign it into law. He hoped that the compromise would bring the country a period of peace and good feeling. Instead, it seemed to increase tensions and hatreds. In 1848 Fillmore was not nominated for the presidency. Southerners were unhappy that California had been admitted as a free state. Northerners were outraged at the provisions of the Fugitive Slave

Millard Fillmore, sworn in as president the day after Taylor's death, threw his support in favor of Clay's compromise and signed the bills that made it up in September 1850.

Act. The four years of Zachary Taylor's term ended on that sour note. Whether Taylor himself could have ended the term on a better note, no one will ever know.

Eight years later, in 1861, the nation finally broke apart. The immediate cause of the breakup was the election of Abraham Lincoln, who had campaigned for Zachary Taylor in 1848. The southern states seceded from the Union and formed the Confederate States of America. They elected as their president Jefferson Davis, Taylor's old friend and former son-in-law.

Fast Facts Zachary Taylor

Birth:	November 24, 1784
Birthplace:	Barboursville, Virginia
Parents:	Richard and Sarah Strother Taylor
Brothers & Sisters:	Hancock (1781–1841)
	William Dabney Strother (1782– ?)
	George (? – ?)
	Elizabeth Lee (1792–1845)
	Joseph Pannill (1796–1864)
	Sarah Bailey (1799– ?)
	Emily Richard (1801– ?)
Education:	No formal education
Occupation:	Military officer, plantation owner
Marriage:	To Margaret "Peggy" Mackall Smith on June 21, 1810
Children:	(*See* "First Lady Fast Facts" at right)
Political Party:	Whig
Public Offices:	1849–1850 Twelfth president of the United States
His Vice President:	Millard Fillmore of New York, who succeeded to the presidency when Taylor died, serving as the 13th president from July 1850 to March 1853
Major Actions as President:	1849 Helped arrange admission of California to the Union as a free (nonslave) state
	1849 Presented a plan for addressing the issue of slavery in new territories
	1850 Signed the Clayton-Bulwer Treaty with Great Britain, in which both countries agreed not to establish new colonies in Central America and to cooperate on plans for a Central American canal linking the Atlantic and Pacific Oceans
Firsts:	First president who never held a previous public office
Death:	July 9, 1850, in the White House, Washington, D.C.
Age at Death:	65 years
Burial Place:	Zachary Taylor National Military Cemetery, Louisville, Kentucky

Fast Facts

Margaret Mackall Smith Taylor

Birth:	September 21, 1788
Birthplace:	Calvert County, Maryland
Parents:	Walter and Ann Mackall Smith
Education:	Not known
Marriage:	To Zachary Taylor on June 21, 1810
Children:	Ann Mackall (1811–1875)
	Sarah Knox (1814–1835)
	Octavia Pannill (1816–1820)
	Margaret Smith (1819–1820)
	Mary Elizabeth "Betty" (1824–1909)
	Richard (1826–1879)
Died:	August 14, 1852
Age at Death:	63 years
Burial Place:	Zachary Taylor Military Cemetery, Louisville, Kentucky

Timeline

1784	1785	1808	1810	1812
Zachary Taylor is born November 24 in Virginia	Taylor family moves to Kentucky region, settles near Louisville	Taylor receives a commission in the U.S. Army	Marries Margaret Mackall Smith	Commands the defense of Fort Harrison (Indiana Territory) in War of 1812

1835	1837	1841	1845	1846
Taylor's daughter Knox dies three months after her marriage to Jefferson Davis	Taylor defeats the Seminole at the Battle of Lake Okeechobee in Florida	Takes command of the army's Second District, including Indian Territory	Ordered to Corpus Christi, Texas, to defend against war threats by Mexico	(January) Builds Fort Texas on the Rio Grande in territory claimed by Mexico and Texas

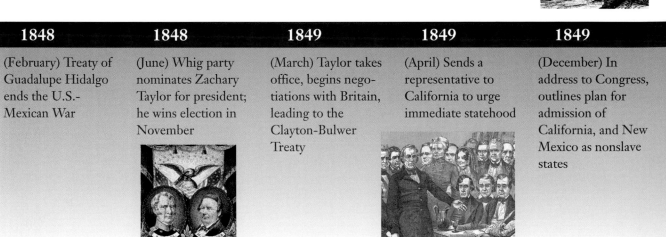

1848	1848	1849	1849	1849
(February) Treaty of Guadalupe Hidalgo ends the U.S.-Mexican War	(June) Whig party nominates Zachary Taylor for president; he wins election in November	(March) Taylor takes office, begins negotiations with Britain, leading to the Clayton-Bulwer Treaty	(April) Sends a representative to California to urge immediate statehood	(December) In address to Congress, outlines plan for admission of California, and New Mexico as nonslave states

1815	1816	1822	1828	1832
War of 1812 ends	Taylor's young daughters Octavia and Margaret die in a fever epidemic	Stationed at Baton Rouge; buys a cotton plantation near the army base	Takes command of Fort Snelling (in present-day Minnesota)	Takes part in the Black Hawk War in present-day Illinois and Wisconsin

1846	1846	1846	1847	1847
(April) A Mexican attack on Taylor's forces causes U.S. to declare war on May 13	(May) Taylor defeats Mexican army at Palo Alto and Resaca de la Palma in present-day Texas; captures Matamoros in Mexico	(September) Taylor attacks and captures Monterrey, Mexico	(March) Outnumbered 4-1, Taylor's troops defeat Mexican army at Buena Vista	(December) With the fighting ended, Taylor returns to hero's welcome in the U.S.

1850	1850
(January–July) Refuses to support Henry Clay's compromise addressing slavery issues	(July) Taylor becomes ill after July Fourth festivities, dies on July 9. Vice President Millard Fillmore becomes president

Glossary

annex: to take a new territory into a city or nation; the United States annexed Texas in 1845

artillery: cannons or other large guns that are operated by artillery crews

battery: an artillery unit

brevet: an honorary military promotion during a war in recognition of heroism; a brevet raises an officer's rank, but not his pay

cavalry: military unit that fights while mounted on horses

fugitive: running away; a fugitive slave is a slave who has escaped from his or her master

gastroenteritis: an inflammation of the lining of the stomach and intestines

infantry: military unit that fights on foot

omnibus bill: in a legislature such as Congress, a bill presented for a vote that includes many different laws or provisions

recruit: a person who has just entered the army, usually at a junior level

regular: a soldier who belongs to the permanent army; not a volunteer who has enlisted for a short time

Further Reading

Collins, David R. *Zachary Taylor, 12th President of the United States*. Ada, OK: Garrett
  Educational Corporation, 1989.

Deem, James M. *Zachary Taylor*. Berkeley Heights, NJ: Enslow Publishers, 2002.

Joseph, Paul. *Zachary Taylor*. Edina, MN: Abdo Publishing Company, 2002.

Kent, Zachary. *Zachary Taylor, Twelfth President of the United States*. Chicago:
  Children's Press, 1988.

Martin, Patricia M. *Zachary Taylor*. New York: Putnam, 1969.

Nardo, Don. *The Mexican-American War*. San Diego: Lucent Books, 1999.

Shaara, Jeff. *Gone for Soldiers: A Novel of the Mexican-American War*. New York:
  Ballantine Books, 2000.

MORE ADVANCED READING

Bauer, K. Jack. *Zachary Taylor: Soldier, Planter, Statesman of the Old Southwest*.
  Newtown, CT: American Political Biography Press, 1994.

Places to Visit

The Pentagon Barracks

Baton Rouge, LA

These barracks, built around 1820, were the center of the base Zachary Taylor commanded three times during his career. Today, they are part of the Louisiana State Capitol complex and house apartments and government offices.

Palo Alto National Historic Site

1623 Central Boulevard, Room 213
Brownsville, TX 78520
(956) 541-2785

The Palo Alto Battlefield, near Brownsville, Texas, is under development. Its offices are in Brownsville, and there is a temporary visitor's center on the site that offers information about the battle and a guide to the battleground.

Zachary Taylor National Cemetery

4701 Brownsboro Road
Louisville, KY 40207
(502) 893-3852

Zachary Taylor and his wife Margaret Taylor are buried here.

United States Capitol

Constitution Avenue
Washington, DC 20510
(202) 224-3121

The Senate chamber was the site of the great debates between Henry Clay, John C. Calhoun, Daniel Webster, and others in 1850 during Taylor's presidency.

White House

1600 Pennsylvania Avenue
Washington, DC 20500
Visitors' Information: (202) 456-7041

During Taylor's time, several White House rooms were redecorated. Taylor died there on July 9, 1850.

Online Sites of Interest

★ **Internet Public Library, Presidents of the United States (IPL-POTUS)**

http://www.ipl.org/div/potus/ztaylor.html

This excellent site offers facts about Zachary Taylor and links to other sites that provide biographies, historical documents, and audio and video files.

★ **Americanpresident.org**

http://www.americanpresident.org/history/zacharytaylor

This site offers a brief thumbnail biography on its opening page and more detailed information about Taylor's early life, military career, and presidency on the following pages.

★ **Palo Alto Battlefield**

http://www.nps.gov/paal

Provides information on the battlefield, which is being developed by the National Park Service, including a description of the battle and directions to the site.

★ **Portraits of the presidents and first ladies**

http://www.memory.loc.gov/ammem/odmdhtml/preshome.html

The Library of Congress provides portraits of the presidents and most first ladies.

★ **The White House**

http://www.whitehouse.gov

Lots of information on the current president and on the White House itself, including a tour of the building and information about presidential pets. To find short biographies of presidents, go to

http://www.whitehouse.gov/history/presidents

★ **National First Ladies' Library**

http://www.firstladies.org

A collection of information on the first ladies, including presidents' wives and others who served officially as White House hostesses. For biographies of the first ladies, go to http://www.firstladies.org/Bibliography.htm

Table of Presidents

1. George Washington   **2. John Adams**   **3. Thomas Jefferson**   **4. James Madison**

Took office	Apr 30 1789	Mar 4 1797	Mar 4 1801	Mar 4 1809
Left office	Mar 3 1797	Mar 3 1801	Mar 3 1809	Mar 3 1817
Birthplace	Westmoreland Co, VA	Braintree, MA	Shadwell, VA	Port Conway, VA
Birth date	Feb 22 1732	Oct 20 1735	Apr 13 1743	Mar 16 1751
Death date	Dec 14 1799	July 4 1826	July 4 1826	June 28 1836

9. William H. Harrison   **10. John Tyler**   **11. James K. Polk**   **12. Zachary Taylor**

Took office	Mar 4 1841	Apr 6 1841	Mar 4 1845	Mar 5 1849
Left office	**Apr 4 1841•**	Mar 3 1845	Mar 3 1849	**July 9 1850•**
Birthplace	Berkeley, VA	Greenway, VA	Mecklenburg Co, NC	Barboursville, VA
Birth date	Feb 9 1773	Mar 29 1790	Nov 2 1795	Nov 24 1784
Death date	Apr 4 1841	Jan 18 1862	June 15 1849	July 9 1850

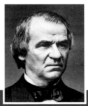    

17. Andrew Johnson   **18. Ulysses S. Grant**   **19. Rutherford B. Hayes**   **20. James A. Garfield**

Took office	Apr 15 1865	Mar 4 1869	Mar 4 1877	Mar 4 1881
Left office	Mar 3 1869	Mar 3 1877	Mar 3 1881	**Sept 19 1881•**
Birthplace	Raleigh, NC	Point Pleasant, OH	Delaware, OH	Orange, OH
Birth date	Dec 29 1808	Apr 27 1822	Oct 4 1822	Nov 19 1831
Death date	July 31 1875	July 23 1885	Jan 17 1893	Sept 19 1881

5. James Monroe	**6. John Quincy Adams**	**7. Andrew Jackson**	**8. Martin Van Buren**
Mar 4 1817	Mar 4 1825	Mar 4 1829	Mar 4 1837
Mar 3 1825	Mar 3 1829	Mar 3 1837	Mar 3 1841
Westmoreland Co, VA	Braintree, MA	The Waxhaws, SC	Kinderhook, NY
Apr 28 1758	July 11 1767	Mar 15 1767	Dec 5 1782
July 4 1831	Feb 23 1848	June 8 1845	July 24 1862

13. Millard Fillmore	**14. Franklin Pierce**	**15. James Buchanan**	**16. Abraham Lincoln**
July 9 1850	Mar 4 1853	Mar 4 1857	Mar 4 1861
Mar 3 1853	Mar 3 1857	Mar 3 1861	**Apr 15 1865•**
Locke Township, NY	Hillsborough, NH	Cove Gap, PA	Hardin Co, KY
Jan 7 1800	Nov 23 1804	Apr 23 1791	Feb 12 1809
Mar 8 1874	Oct 8 1869	June 1 1868	Apr 15 1865

21. Chester A. Arthur	**22. Grover Cleveland**	**23. Benjamin Harrison**	**24. Grover Cleveland**
Sept 19 1881	Mar 4 1885	Mar 4 1889	Mar 4 1893
Mar 3 1885	Mar 3 1889	Mar 3 1893	Mar 3 1897
Fairfield, VT	Caldwell, NJ	North Bend, OH	Caldwell, NJ
Oct 5 1830	Mar 18 1837	Aug 20 1833	Mar 18 1837
Nov 18 1886	June 24 1908	Mar 13 1901	June 24 1908

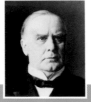

	25. William McKinley	**26. Theodore Roosevelt**	**27. William H. Taft**	**28. Woodrow Wilson**
Took office	Mar 4 1897	Sept 14 1901	Mar 4 1909	Mar 4 1913
Left office	**Sept 14 1901•**	Mar 3 1909	Mar 3 1913	Mar 3 1921
Birthplace	Niles, OH	New York, NY	Cincinnati, OH	Staunton, VA
Birth date	Jan 29 1843	Oct 27 1858	Sept 15 1857	Dec 28 1856
Death date	Sept 14 1901	Jan 6 1919	Mar 8 1930	Feb 3 1924

	33. Harry S. Truman	**34. Dwight D. Eisenhower**	**35. John F. Kennedy**	**36. Lyndon B. Johnson**
Took office	Apr 12 1945	Jan 20 1953	Jan 20 1961	Nov 22 1963
Left office	Jan 20 1953	Jan 20 1961	**Nov 22 1963•**	Jan 20 1969
Birthplace	Lamar, MO	Denison, TX	Brookline, MA	Johnson City, TX
Birth date	May 8 1884	Oct 14 1890	May 29 1917	Aug 27 1908
Death date	Dec 26 1972	Mar 28 1969	Nov 22 1963	Jan 22 1973

	41. George Bush	**42. Bill Clinton**	**43. George W. Bush**	
Took office	Jan 20 1989	Jan 20 1993	Jan 20 2001	
Left office	Jan 20 1993	Jan 20 2001	—	
Birthplace	Milton, MA	Hope, AR	New Haven, CT	
Birth date	June 12 1924	Aug 19 1946	July 6 1946	
Death date	—	—	—	

29. Warren G. Harding

Mar 4 1921

Aug 2 1923•

Blooming Grove, OH

Nov 21 1865

Aug 2 1923

30. Calvin Coolidge

Aug 2 1923

Mar 3 1929

Plymouth, VT

July 4 1872

Jan 5 1933

31. Herbert Hoover

Mar 4 1929

Mar 3 1933

West Branch, IA

Aug 10 1874

Oct 20 1964

32. Franklin D. Roosevelt

Mar 4 1933

Apr 12 1945•

Hyde Park, NY

Jan 30 1882

Apr 12 1945

37. Richard M. Nixon

Jan 20 1969

Aug 9 1974★

Yorba Linda, CA

Jan 9 1913

Apr 22 1994

38. Gerald R. Ford

Aug 9 1974

Jan 20 1977

Omaha, NE

July 14 1913

—

39. Jimmy Carter

Jan 20 1977

Jan 20 1981

Plains, GA

Oct 1 1924

—

40. Ronald Reagan

Jan 20 1981

Jan 20 1989

Tampico, IL

Feb 11 1911

—

• Indicates the president died while in office.

★ Richard Nixon resigned before his term expired.

Index

★ ★ ★ ★ ★

Page numbers in *italics* indicate illustrations.

abolitionists, 56
Alligator (Native American chief), 33
American Revolution, 10, 11
Appalachian Mountains, 10
Arista, Mariano, 40, 42
Arkansas, 37
"Army of Occupation," *39*
arsenic, 91
Atkinson, Henry, 28

Bad Axe, Battle of, 30, *31*
Baton Rouge, Louisiana, *24*, 25, 53, 62
Beargrass Creek, 10, *12*, 18, 23
Belknap, William, 45
Benton, Thomas Hart, 82, 89
Black Hawk (Sac and Fox leader), 28, 30
Black Hawk War, 28–30, *31*
Bliss, William, 64, 75, *76*
Buena Vista, Battle of, 7, 8, *9*, 48, *49*, 50, *55*
Buffalo, New York, 61
Butler, William, 57

Calhoun, John C., 78, 79–80, *80*
California, 69, 70, *72*, *73*, 74, 77, 79, 93
cartoon, political, *61, 63, 82*
Cass, Lewis, 57, 62, 64
Central America, 69
Cherokee tribe, 29
Chickasaw tribe, 29
Choctaw tribe, 29
Civil War, 92
Clay, Henry, 50, 56, 60, 78–79, *78*, 80, 81,
        83, 85, 91–92, 93
Clayton, John, 69
Clayton-Bulwer Treaty, 69–70, 86, 92

Compromise of 1850, 92
Confederate States of America, 95
Congress, 40, 55, 56, 57, 70, 74, 78–81, 82,
        82, 85, 86–87, 93
Corpus Christi, Texas, 38–39, *39*
cotton, 14, *15*, 56
Creek tribe, 29
Crittenden, John, 62
Croghan, George, 11
Cumberland Gap, 10

Davis, Jefferson, 30, 32–33, *32*, 75, 81, 87,
        95
Democratic party, 57, 59, 62, 67
Dixon's Ferry, 28, 30
Duncan, James, 43

El Salvador, 69

Falls of the Ohio, 10
Fillmore, Millard, *58*, 60, 91, 93, *94*
fire-eaters, 56
Florida Territory, 33
Foote, Henry, 85
Fort Crawford (Wisconsin), 27, 30
Fort Harrison (Indiana), 19–20, *21*
Fort Smith (Arkansas), 37
Fort Snelling (Minnesota), 25, *26*
Fort Texas, *41*, 42
Fox tribe, 28, 30
Free Soil party, 62, 80, 82
Fugitive Slave Act, 78, 79, 93–94

Ghent, Treaty of, 20, *22*
gold rush, 70, *72*, *73*
Great Britain, 19, 69, 92
Guadalupe Hidalgo, Treaty of, 46

Hawthorne, Nathaniel, 67
Honduras, 69
The House of Seven Gables, 67
House of Representatives, 55, 56, 57

Indian Removal Act, 29
Indian Territory, 33
Indiana Territory, 19, *21*

Jackson, Andrew, 20, 22, 29
Jefferson, Thomas, 29
Jones, Sam (Native American chief), 33

Kentucky, 10, 11, *12*, 13, 16, 18, 88
King, Thomas Butler, 70

Lake Okeechobee, Battle of, 33
Lincoln, Abraham, 55, 64, 67, 91, 95
Louisiana, 24, 25, 53, 62
Louisville, Kentucky, *12*, 13, 16, 18, 88

Matamoros, Mexico, *41*, 45
Maysville, Kentucky, 16
Mexico, 7–8, 38, 39, 40, *41*, 43, 45, 46, 47,
    48, 50, 52, 81
Mexico City, Mexico, 47, 48, 50, 52
Monroe, James, 69
Monterrey, Battle of, 7–8, 46, 47, 48

Native Americans, 13, 19, 20, 25, 28–30,
    33–34, 38, 69
New Mexico, 74, 77, 79, 85
New Orleans, Louisiana, 53
New York, 59
Nicaragua, 69, 92
Nueces River, 39

Old Whitey (horse), 42, 46, 53, 75, 88, *90*
omnibus bill, 81, 83, 91–92

Oregon Territory, 69

Palo Alto, Battle of, 42–43, *44*
Pentagon Barracks, *24*
Polk, James K., 38, 40, 46, 57
"popular sovereignty," 57
Prairie du Chien, Wisconsin, 27
Proviso, Wilmot, 62

Resaca de la Palma, Battle of, 45
Ringgold, Sam, 43
Rio Grande (river), 39, 40, *41*, 45

Sac tribe, 28–29, 30
San Juan, Nicaragua, 69
Santa Anna, Antonio López de, 7, 48, 50
Santa Fe County, New Mexico, 74, 79, 85
The Scarlet Letter, 67
Scott, Winfield, 47, 51, 52, 60, 88
Seminole tribe, 29, 33–34
Senate, 56, 78–81, 82, *82*, 86–87
Seneca Falls, New York, 59
Seward, William, 64, 67–68, *68*, 77, 81
Shawnee tribe, 20
Sierra Madre (mountain range), *49*
slavery, 13, 14, *15*, 25, 35, 38, 55, 56, 60–62,
    65, 68, 70, 74, 77–78, 79, 81, 85, 93–94
Smith, Margaret Mackall. *See* Taylor,
    Margaret Mackall Smith.
Springfield estate, 10, *12*, 13
states during Taylor's presidency, map of, *71*

Tampa Bay, Florida, 33
Taylor, Ann Mackall (daughter), 19, 23, 25,
    27, 52, 75, 87
Taylor, Dabney (grandson), 91
Taylor, Elizabeth (sister), 11
Taylor, George (brother), 11
Taylor, Hancock (brother), 11

Taylor, Margaret (daughter), 23

Taylor, Margaret Mackall Smith (wife), *17*, 18, 23, 25, 75, 87
    fast facts, 97

Taylor, Mary Elizabeth "Betty" (daughter), 25, 64, 75, 87

Taylor, Octavia (daughter), 23

Taylor, Richard (father), 10, 13, 92

Taylor, Richard (son), 25

Taylor, Sarah Knox (daughter), 23, 30, 32–33

Taylor, William (brother), 11

Taylor, Zachary, *54, 58, 61, 66, 76, 84, 90*
    "Army of Occupation," *39*
    at Battle of Bad Axe, 30
    at Battle of Buena Vista, 7–8, 48, 50, 55
    at Battle of Palo Alto, 42–43, 45
    birth of, 10
    childhood of, 11
    commander of Fort Snelling, 25
    commander of Second Military District, 37–38
    death of, 87–88, *87*, 91
    education of, 11
    election of 1848, 62, 64
    fast facts, 96
    foreign affairs and, 92
    at Fort Crawford, 27
    at Fort Harrison, 19, 20, 22
    at Fort Texas, 40
    "hero of Buena Vista," 53, *54*
    inauguration of, 65–67, *66*
    marriage, 18
    modern views of, 89, 91–93
    nickname, 8
    plantation owner, 23, 34–35
    president, 69, 70, 74–75, 77, 83, 85, 86, 89
    presidential candidate, 57, *58*, 60, *61*, 62, *63*, 64

Taylor, Zachary (cont'd)
    Seminole Indians and, 33–34
    U.S.-Mexican War, 42–43, 45, 46–48, 50, 52

Taylor, Zachary, Jr. (uncle), 11

Tecumseh (Shawnee leader), 20

telegraph, 8

Terre Haute, Indiana, *21*

Texas, 38–39, *39*, 40
    battles in, 42–43, *44*, 45, 46

Thornton, Seth, 40

tobacco, 14

"Trail of Tears," 29

Tyler, John, 38

U.S.-Mexican War, 40, 42–43, *44*, 47–48, *49*, 50, 52, 62
    fast facts, 46

Van Buren, Martin, 62, 64

Veracruz, Mexico, 46, 52

voting rights, 59

War of 1812, 19–20, 22
    fast facts, 20

Washington, George, 14, 46

Washington Monument, 85

Webster, Daniel, 78, 80–81, *81*, 86–87

Weed, Thurlow, 83

Whig party, 53, 57, *58*, 59, 60, 62, 67, 83

White House, 77

Whitman, Walt, 46

Whitney, Eli, 14

Wild Cat (Native American chief), 33

Wilmot, David, 55

Wilmot Proviso, 55, 57

women's rights, 59

Wood, Robert, 25, 27

About the Author

Deborah Kops has written eight other nonfiction books for children, including *Abraham Lincoln* and *The Battle of Bull Run*. Her work has appeared in many newspapers and magazines, among them *The New York Times*, *Boston Globe*, *Vermont Life*, and *Country Journal*. Kops graduated from the University of Michigan and holds a master's degree in education from Antioch-Putney graduate school. She lives with her husband and son in the Greater Boston area.